THE PRINCIPLES
OF OUR WORLD
™

A collection of stories about how the
PRINCIPLE OF HOPE
can help us along the journey of life

Written by
David Esposito

HOPE

Independently published by Harvest Time Partners, Inc.
www.harvesttimepartners.com

Layout and illustrations by Imbue, The Marketing Agency at Digital Dog Direct.
www.imbuecreative.com

For additional information and permissions, please contact:
Harvest Time Partners, Inc.
Attention: David Anthony Esposito
Email: david@harvesttimepartners.com
Phone: 1-877-786-4278 or 269-370-9275

Harvest Time Partners, Inc.
ISBN-13: 978-0692263389 (Custom Universal)
ISBN-10: 0692263381

*Dedicated to my Mom and Dad,
Mabel and Anthony Esposito.*

*Thank you for giving me the gift of a
strong foundation. It has meant more
than you will ever know.*

About the Author

David Esposito is a combat veteran, business executive, husband, father, and creator of character-building resources that help individuals, families, and organizations reach their full potential.

He has developed award-winning resources under the brand Character Creates Opportunity®, a character-development initiative designed for all ages. He is also the inventor of Abundant Harvest® and Face to Face®: award-winning conversation games that are being utilized in families, schools, counseling programs, and faith-based organizations worldwide. The games help families and educators open the door to more effective communication and encourage decision making based on principles such as honesty, loyalty, and commitment with the intent of reinforcing the law of the harvest, simply, you "reap what you sow." Abundant Harvest and Face to Face help foster effective conversations on real-world issues and develop the critical life skill of face-to-face communication that is rapidly being replaced by today's online chatter.

David's character and leadership skills were cultivated at West Point and through leadership assignments in the US Army Infantry. As an airborne ranger infantry officer, David led a rifle platoon with the 101st Airborne Division through several combat operations in the Gulf War. He was recognized with a Bronze Star for combat operations in February 1991.

After launching his business career as a top sales representative, David quickly rose through the ranks of corporate America advancing to become the president of a $100-million-plus medical diagnostics company.

David and his wife Tracy founded and sponsor the Harvest Time Partners Foundation, a charitable organization that supports children and young adults in the pursuit of character-building opportunities worldwide. The Foundation supports a wide range of initiatives from college scholarships to community-service projects, as well as international efforts to reduce the suffering of children and young adults.

David provides support to individuals, families, and organizations on a variety of topics and subjects encompassing personal and executive development, team building, leadership training, and building a strong marriage and family. You can contact him at david@harvesttimepartners.com or by calling (877) 786-4278.

Visit www.harvesttimepartners.com to learn more.

What's Inside?

A Note to Parents and Teachers in the Home, the School, and the Community

There is no greater impact that we can make in this world than guiding children to develop the skills and abilities to most effectively handle life's ups and downs. Children are the builders of the future for our families and society, and we need to give them the best tools possible.

As much as we would like to "protect" children from the challenges of this world, the reality is that we cannot protect them forever. We would be wise to focus our efforts on preparation rather than protection in order to prepare them for the unavoidable reality that they will encounter challenges during their journey through life.

Aristotle wrote, "Good habits formed at youth make all the difference."

We have a responsibility as parents and teachers to help children form good habits and give them one of the greatest gifts: a strong foundation for living. A foundation that will support them in effectively dealing with the situations they will encounter in life.

There will always be new ideas and new techniques to support us in our changing world. However, even as techniques may change, we need consistent reminders that principles like honesty, loyalty, and commitment will remain the most effective foundation to form our decisions and actions, regardless of the changes in the world around us.

Our hope is that this book will be a helpful reminder to you and the children in your care about the importance of **The Principles** of honesty, teamwork, compassion, courage, and so many others.

The Principles can act as a compass to guide us through all the situations we encounter in life.

The Principles help individuals build and strengthen their character and *Character Creates Opportunity*® for a successful life, regardless of our situation.

There is a moment of time between our situation and how we respond.
In that moment of time, we have complete freedom to choose our response.
*The **inner voice** that drives our response is our **character.***

__The Principles__ arrive in that moment of time to help guide our response
based on a principle like honesty, compassion, and loyalty,
*which will build and strengthen our **character**.*

__The Principles__ bring truth and lend strength to our inner voice.

As you use this book to help build a strong foundation in children, we hope it also serves
as a good reminder to you about the importance of living a life according to principles.

A Note to Children

Life is an exciting journey filled with fun, excitement, wonder, and, sometimes, struggles and challenges.

Have you ever ridden a roller coaster?

Life is like riding a roller coaster.

There is so much excitement in the beginning as you get ready to jump in the seat and start the ride. We all must buckle up for safety as the roller coaster will have many ups and downs, twists and turns; so buckling up is the smart thing to do.

There will be times when you will be so high on the roller coaster that you can see everything that is all around you. You will see the exciting turns ahead, and you will know exactly what is coming next.

Then, all of a sudden, you will be in a dark tunnel and a little bit scared because you cannot see what is in front of you.

Then, you speed out of the tunnel into the light again. You're back to enjoying the twists and turns and ups and downs once again.

Life is like a roller coaster ride. This book was written to help prepare you for the "roller coaster" of life.

In this book, you will learn about **The Principles**.

The Principles will help keep you safe during the ups and downs and twists and turns of life, just like the seat belt on the roller coaster.

The Principles will always be at your side to help you during the greatest roller coaster ride—your LIFE!

Now, get ready to buckle up with **The Principles.** Have fun!

The Principle of Hope

"Hello, I am The Principle of Hope.

"People say I am the reminder they need to keep believing in their dreams even when they are unsure of what tomorrow will bring.

"People also say that I am the helpful hand that pulls them out of a struggle.

"There will be times in your life when you struggle to accomplish your goals. I will help give you strength to believe in yourself, so you can keep making progress toward your goals.

"My parents told me that when they were young and newly married, all they had was Hope; and that is why they named me Hope.

"Please call on me when you need a 'light' to get through a dark struggle. I will help remind you that you can achieve your dreams no matter how difficult today may seem.

"I will be there to support and encourage you—no matter what situations you experience in life.

"Please, count on me to help you have Hope when you are struggling."

Hope in Our Home

Charlie and his younger brother Matthew had a wonderful time playing in the yard with their dog Sparky. Sparky had been a part of their family ever since the boys were born, and they loved playing with him out in the yard.

However, today was different. When the boys were playing with Sparky in the morning, the dog saw a squirrel and chased after it into the woods. Sparky ran so fast that the boys could not catch him.

The boys and their parents spent most of the day searching the neighborhood looking for Sparky.

It was now late in the evening, and Sparky still had not returned home. Everyone was sad and tired.

Charlie, Matthew, and their mom and dad stood at the window hoping to see Sparky come running back to the house.

"Boys, it is time to go bed," said Charlie and Matthew's mom. Charlie was very upset about Sparky running away. Sparky had slept outside his bedroom door ever since he was a little baby. Charlie always felt safe with Sparky by his door when he was sleeping.

In a moment of time, a number of thoughts raced through Charlie's mind.

Charlie thought: "I am so sad that Sparky has not come home. He always protected our family at night. I am very scared without him in our home.

"I don't know what I will do without him. I sure hope Sparky comes back home."

"Everyone gets a little sad and worried in a situation like this—especially when you don't know how things will turn out in the end," said The Principle of Hope. "I know how much you love Sparky and enjoy having him by your door to protect you at night while you are sleeping.

"However, as The Principle of Hope, I want to tell you that you know Sparky is a really smart dog. He knows how to find his way home. I am sure you remember the time last winter when he was lost in the snowstorm. He found his way back home then. Because he did it before, I am sure he will find his way home again now.

"The right thing to do is to be full of the Hope that he will return home like he always has before."

In that moment of time, Charlie thought about what The Principle of Hope said about believing that Sparky will do what he has done before: return home. With that in mind, Charlie decided what to do.

Charlie looked around at his family and said, "Hey guys, I know we are all sad that Sparky has not returned home yet. However, Sparky is a super-smart dog; and he has always returned home after he ran away. When he gets hungry and tired, he always finds his way home—no matter how far away he goes."

Charlie's reminder about how Sparky always returned home in the past brought some Hope into everyone's hearts that Sparky would return home again soon.

Just as Charlie and Matthew were turning to walk upstairs to bed, their dad shouted, "Hey, I think I see Sparky running up the driveway!"

Sure enough, Sparky returned home again just like before when he was hungry and tired.

The Principle of Hope helped remind Charlie that remembering how things turned out in the past can help pull you out of a struggle today.

Later that evening, as Charlie lay in bed ready to go to sleep, The Principle of Hope came to his bedside.

The Principle of Hope said, "Charlie, I am really glad that you chose to believe Sparky would return home again just like he did so many other times before.

"I know you were sad and worried, but you did the right thing by having Hope that he would return home.

"Please remember that Hope can always pull you out of a struggle when you encounter similar situations in life."

Hope in Our School

Sally is in the fourth grade. On one particular day, Sally was very worried because she had to take a difficult science test at the end of the day. She had been studying hard all week for the test because the teacher said that it would be the hardest test of the year.

The entire class was nervous about taking the test because they knew it was going to be a challenge.

Sally found it very difficult to be happy during the day because she kept thinking about the test she needed to take at the end of the day.

During lunchtime, Sally was usually smiling and talking to her friends. However, today she sat quietly. Because she was so worried about the test, she did not even eat any of her lunch.

Sally felt like she had "butterflies" in her stomach, and she started to feel like she was going to be sick.

In a moment of time, a number of thoughts raced through Sally's mind.

Sally thought to herself: "I know this test is going to be so hard. I am starting to feel sick to my stomach, and I can't even eat my lunch. I studied hard all week for the test, but I am just so scared that I will not do well on the test."

"Everyone gets a little scared when they have to take a difficult test," said The Principle of Hope. "Sometimes we all get so worried that we can't eat and don't feel like talking to anyone. In addition, science is a very hard class; and I know how much you want to do well on the test.

"However, as The Principle of Hope, I want to tell you that you know how hard you studied all week for this test. You studied more for this test than any other test that you have taken in school.

"Sally, you have always studied hard for tests in the past; and you get very good grades because of the hard work and effort you put into your studies.

"As difficult as this test will be, I think you should feel really good about how well you prepared—that should help you do very well on the science test."

Sally, I will be right by your side as you get ready for the test.

In that moment of time, Sally thought about what The Principle of Hope said about how hard she studied for the test and how that hard work will always help her do well on tests in school.

Sally began to feel better in her stomach, and it seemed like her "butterflies" just flew away. Sally also decided to eat some of her lunch because she knew the food would give her the energy she needed to take the test. She even began to smile and talk with her friends.

At the end of the day, the class took the science test. Sally worked hard and gave her best effort on the test.

Sally stayed around after class to receive her grade from the teacher. The teacher smiled at Sally and said, "Just like on other tests Sally, you did great on this one: A+!"

The Principle of Hope helped remind Sally about how studying hard can always help you do well on tests in school, even in science class!

Later that evening, as Sally lay in bed ready to go to sleep, The Principle of Hope came to her bedside.

The Principle of Hope said, "Sally, I am really glad that you studied hard for the test, and you remembered that studying hard will always help you do well on hard tests in school.

"I know you will continue to work hard in school, and that should always give you Hope that you will do well on tests.

"Please remember that hard work, and Hope can always help you overcome your fears in school."

Sally, you can sleep well tonight because you did the right thing today.

Hope in Our Parents

Jim and Janice had twin six-year-old boys, Ryan and Tyler. Jim recently lost his job; and he was having a difficult time finding a new one. Janice was working; but with two growing boys, Jim needed to find a job soon so they could provide for their growing family.

Today was an exciting and scary morning. A new factory opened in town. The company will be making electric cars. Jim was going to the new factory to see if he could get a job.

Jim was excited about the chance to get a really great job. However, he was also a little scared because he knew there were only a few jobs in the factory; and a lot of people want the jobs.

"Janice," Jim spoke softly. "I really need to find work. You know I have been looking everywhere, and I just have not been able to find a good job. This car factory could be a great job for me, but I know there are so many other people trying to find work in the new factory."

Janice stood quietly listening to Jim worry about the day.

In a moment of time, a number of thoughts raced through Janice's mind.

Janice thought: "If Jim could get this job, we really could take care of our growing boys. Jim is really smart, and he is a hard worker. He has always done well in the past, but I know there are so many other people trying to get these great new jobs. I don't know what to say."

"Everyone gets quiet and is not sure what to say in times like this," said The Principle of Hope. "Jim has a big day today, and I know you want to say something that will be helpful. The whole family is counting on Jim to get a job.

"However, as The Principle of Hope, I want to tell you that you know Jim is very smart; and he always works hard. That new factory needs people like Jim to build those great cars. Even though there are a lot of other people looking for jobs, Jim has done well in the past; and he will do well in the future.

"As difficult as this time is for your family, the most helpful thing to do now is to fill Jim with Hope; so that he will believe he can get this great job and provide for your growing family."

In that moment of time, Janice thought about what The Principle of Hope said about Jim being a hard worker and that the new factory would need some people like Jim. She was reminded about how Jim did well in the past, and that would help him do well in the future.

Janice looked at Jim with a big smile and said, "Jim, I know you are worried about what will happen today; but you should remember that you are smart and a hard worker. The new factory needs a person like you. You have done so well in the past; I know you are going to do well again today."

Jim left the house feeling very good about reaching his goal of getting a job in the new factory.

Later in the evening when the kids came back from school and Janice came home from work, Jim had some exciting news to tell them. "I got the job!" Jim shouted and jumped for joy.

The Principle of Hope helped remind Janice and Jim about believing they can reach their goals, no matter how difficult of a challenge they are facing.

Later that evening, as Janice lay in bed ready to go to sleep, The Principle of Hope came to her bedside.

The Principle of Hope said, "Janice, I am really glad that you reminded Jim that he is smart and a hard worker, and that he would be perfect for a job in the new factory.

"It was important to help Jim leave the house full of Hope about getting the new job even though there were so many other people trying to get the same job.

"Please remember that Hope and hard work are a good mix to help you achieve your goals."

Hope in Our Work

Robert's mother Suzie is a baker. She has her own store, Suzie's Sweet Shop, where she sells cakes, cookies, and all sorts of sweet treats to eat.

Early one Friday morning, a man came running into the store.

"I need a great big chocolate cake ready before the end of today," the man said. "It is for my wife's 40th birthday, and I totally forgot to order the cake earlier in the week. Our party is tonight!"

Suzie knew she already had a full list of cakes and cookies to make today, but she wanted to help this man who forgot to order his wife's birthday cake.

Suzie said, "Sure, I will have the perfect chocolate cake ready for you at 5:00 PM tonight."

"Great! Thank you," said the man. "This is a really special birthday for my wife, so please do your best."

The man quickly ran out the door to get to work on time.

In a moment of time, a number of thoughts raced through Suzie's mind.

Suzie thought to herself: "Wow! This is going to be a rough day. I have so many cakes and cookies to bake already. It is really going to be a challenge to make the chocolate cake in time. Also, this is a special birthday celebration for the man and his wife. I really need to make the perfect cake for their big celebration. I am really worried about how this day is going to turn out."

"When things get real busy, everyone struggles with feeling like they may not be able to get it all done," said The Principle of Hope. "You have a lot of cakes and cookies to bake today, and the man needs a real-special cake for his big celebration.

"However, as The Principle of Hope, I want to tell you that you know you have had many days like this in the past. You are really terrific at making a great plan for busy days like this one. You are a really fast worker which will help get all the cakes and cookies completed on time for today.

"As difficult as today will be, you should be filled with Hope that you will get it all done because you have done this before and have always been able to make it all come together just fine."

In that moment of time, Suzie thought about what The Principle of Hope said about how she had always been terrific at making a great plan to bake all the cakes and cookies. Somehow, she always figured a way to reach her baking goals on some really busy days.

Suzie thought to herself: "I know it will be a super-busy day today. However, if I can make a good plan, I am sure I can also make a special cake for the man and his wife."

Suzie began to list all the cake and cookie projects for the day.

"I am not getting anything done just standing here worrying," Suzie thought to herself. "It is time to get busy!"

The day passed so quickly as Suzie was busy from start to finish. She felt great as she got everything done and also made a great chocolate cake for the special birthday party.

The Principle of Hope helped remind Suzie to keep believing in herself to accomplish her goals no matter how difficult things may seem to be.

Later that evening, Suzie came home from a long day at work. She was very tired; and as she got ready to go to sleep, The Principle of Hope came to her bedside.

The Principle of Hope said, "Suzie, I am really glad that you believed in yourself today and reached your goals for a real-busy day.

"You will face some busy days in the future, and it will be important for you to be filled with Hope that you can get it all done because you have done it so many times in the past.

"Please remember that hard work and Hope can help you continue to reach your goals."

Suzie, you can sleep well tonight because you did the right thing today.

Where Do We Go from Here?

"Hello, again. It is me, The Principle of Hope.

"I trust you enjoyed reading about the different situations in life, and how I can help you reach your goals even when they seem out of reach.

"I want to encourage you to keep Hope alive and by your side every day of your life. Just like practicing your favorite sport or playing your favorite instrument, keeping Hope in your thoughts will help you grow stronger in your ability to reach your goals and overcome challenges.

"As you get older, the situations in life will get harder; and you will need Hope to help you get through some tough situations.

"On the next page of this book, there are some situations where you can practice having Hope to help prepare you for the times when you encounter these situations in your life.

"Please call on me when you need Hope to achieve your goals.

"I will be there to support and encourage you—no matter what situations you experience in life.

"Please, count on me to help you have Hope when you are struggling."

What Would <u>YOU</u> Do?

We will all experience some situations in life when we should choose to remember The Principle of Hope.

Below are some situations to think about how you would respond.

Remember **The Principle of Hope**

"What would YOU do?"

Your family dog is getting old and needs surgery on his knee, so he can walk without pain. Your family is worried about the dog having surgery. What would YOU do?	Your family just moved to a new town. You and your sister will be starting school in a few weeks. You notice that your sister is very worried and scared about going to a new school. What would YOU do?
You have been working hard practicing basketball all summer long to get ready for the tryouts for the school basketball team. You are a little worried about how many people are trying out for the team. What would YOU do?	As you get up for school in the morning, you realize that you forgot that you have a major math test today. What would YOU do?
Your older brother and sister seem to be arguing all the time. It is making everyone sad. What would YOU do?	Your family has planted a nice garden in the spring and have been trying to take care of it all summer long. You are all a little worried about what kind of "harvest" you will have in the fall. What would YOU do?

Some Additional Resources to Help
Award-Winning Conversation Games

As our world has become more connected with things like the internet, smart phones, and social media, today's online chatter has actually caused our families to become more disconnected; and we are losing the critical life-skill of effective face to face communication.

Harvest Time Partners created a series of conversation games called Abundant Harvest® and Face to Face® to help families and educators open the door to more effective communication and encourage decision making based on principles such as honesty and loyalty with the intent of reinforcing the Law of the Harvest, simply, "you reap what you sow." Abundant Harvest and Face to Face conversation games provide parents and teachers with teachable moments and quality time with their children.

Spend quality time discussing real-world situations with your children and students!

Having a difficult time getting teenagers to "open-up" about dealing with their reality? Abundant Harvest for Teens & Adults can help!

Start great conversations with Face to Face, a fast paced, travel ready conversation game!

Kids Edition

For ages 7 and up

Teen Edition

For teenagers 13 and up

Dinner Party Edition

For ages 18 and up, adults and parents

Visit www.harvesttimepartners.com to learn more!

Some Additional Resources to Help
The Principles of Our World Children's Books

The Principle of Honesty	The Principle of Teamwork	The Principle of Sacrifice	The Principle of Courage	The Principle of Compassion
"People say that I am the reminder they need to remain truthful in all that they say and do."	"People say that I am the reminder they need to work together to accomplish great things."	"People say that I am the reminder they need to think about others instead of themselves."	"People say that I am the reminder they need to be brave when they feel worried and afraid."	"People say that I am the reminder they need to reach out to help people in need."

 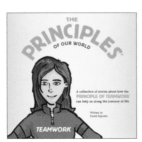   

Visit www.harvesttimepartners.com to learn more!

CPSIA information can be obtained at www.ICGtesting.com
Printed in the USA
LVOW01s2352071114

412606LV00003B/15/P